BATIK FOR BEGINNERS

BERYL MARTIN

BATIK FOR BEGINNERS

ANGUS AND ROBERTSON

Uniform with this book
LET'S MAKE A MOSAIC by June Tanner

First published in 1971 *by*

ANGUS & ROBERTSON LTD

221 George Street, Sydney
54 Bartholomew Close, London
107 Elizabeth Street, Melbourne
89 Anson Road, Singapore

© *Beryl Martin* 1971

National Library of Australia
card number and ISBN 0 207 12167 2

Printed in Singapore by Times Printers Sdn. Bhd.

ACKNOWLEDGMENTS

Grateful thanks are due to the following people who have helped in the preparation of this book: Dr P. G. Martin, who worked with skill and patience to provide the bulk of the photographs; Mark Moody, *Hemisphere* Asian-Australian Magazine, the Indonesian Embassy, Canberra, Messrs Hoechst Ltd, and Chuah Thean Teng and *The Straits Times* for other photographs; Dr Jenny Barker for her assistance, and Susan and Andrew Barker, who helped to make the Christmas Tree; Mrs Lenna Symons, who designed the child's dress and hat; my daughter Amanda, who designed the short skirt; Angela and Michel Smith and Catherine Fleming, who acted as models; and Professor Max Clark, Mrs Edna Pipe, Dr Ravindar Sawhney and Mrs Catherine Verco for the loan of traditional batiks and tools.

B. M.

CONTENTS

1 WHAT IS BATIK?

Have you heard people say that oil and water won't mix? The basis of the batik process of printing on cloth is just as simple as that.

If you have ever tried to write with ink on greasy paper, you will know that the ink will not penetrate over the grease. Probably, in some such accidental way, about two thousand years ago, it was found that if waxy lines were drawn on white cloth which was then dipped in cold-water dye, the parts under the wax remained white—that is, they *resisted* the dye. This, then, became a simple, inexpensive way of producing patterns on fabric that even the poorest people could use to decorate their clothing. This 'resist method', as it is called, used natural raw materials at hand such as beeswax, fat, rice flour, plant resins and vegetable dyes.

The actual origin of batik is shrouded by the veil of time, but archaeologists have discovered evidence that Egyptians and Persians wore batiked garments two thousand years ago. So, too, did the inhabitants of Japan, China, India and most Eastern countries. It is interesting to find that in India, a pattern resembling the ancient paisley design of Scotland has existed for centuries. The Chinese found the resist process a perfect medium for depicting their ornate, delicate designs; in Africa, certain repetitive tribal motifs have been passed down for generations.

But it is in the Indonesian Archipelago, on the island of Java, that the art has reached its highest peak of development. There is evidence that batik existed here as early as the tenth century A.D., and since that time it has become so closely interwoven with the history and culture of the Javanese as to be virtually inseparable from it. This is very largely due to the part played by royalty in the development of batik in Java; one sultan in particular, who reigned in the seventeenth century, so loved the art that he created many of the loveliest designs still extant today. Throughout the courts of Java, batik became the favourite pastime of the ladies, who refined and developed their individual styles. Noble families evolved their own motifs, just as English nobility chose their crests, and the Scottish clans their tartans. Sultans, courtiers, and servants were required to wear these special designs embodying the motifs, under threat of serious punishment if they disobeyed. One pattern, known as *Parang Rusak*, could be worn only by the king himself. Today, this pattern has been debased and is sold in dress-lengths. It is, however, one of the more expensive, hand-drawn patterns, and usually shows some variation of the original (see opposite page).

Through the centuries, various aspects of Javanese history have been embodied in batik designs; and they are rich in religious and mystic symbolism. From the moment of birth, a Javanese baby is wrapped in one particular cloth to protect it from evil spirits. Other patterns are believed to hold the power

2

Parang Rusak design—the Royal design, based on handles of daggers, from the Court of Djokjakarta

to cure illness, and one very ancient design must be drawn only by old women, to ensure its purity, before it is used as part of a traditional offering to the Goddess of the South Seas. Bridal couples and their parents have their special batik patterns, too. Bride and bridegroom wear a pattern known as 'Glory unto you'.

In all these designs, the influence of nature is paramount: they abound with flowers, fish, birds and vines. With the advent of the Islamic religion to Java in the fifteenth century, another interesting influence was added to batik design. No direct representation of man or creature is permitted by this faith, so art had to find a way to circumvent this law. This it did by stylizing the animal or bird, and interweaving an intricate pattern of flowers and leaves around it (see illustrations, p. 5).

As well as being used as a means of identifying people according to their rank and status, the distinctive designs and dyes indigenous to certain regions or ethnic groups made it possible to tell where they came from. Today this still applies: the Sunda-

3

nese of West Java like bold design inspired by Chinese or Hindu motifs—dragons, the phoenix, elephants, tigers and lotus flowers, for example. Central Javanese, still largely under the influence of court taste, prefer more subtle colour combinations of indigo blue, brown and creamy white with fine-drawn patterns. People of the northern plains wear Chinese- or European-inspired designs which are almost *art noveau,* in line with recent world trends.

Individual taste and temperament play their part, too, so that colour, size of pattern and its arrangement may be varied within any single category of batik.

THE TJANTING

The most important factor in the refining of batik design has been the *tjanting,* an implement consisting of a small copper cup with one or more spouts and a handle of bamboo. Its function is to apply molten wax to the fabric. The *tjanting* was introduced in Java in the seventeenth century. Today, the finest batiks are still drawn with the *tjanting,* but the work is laborious, a single piece of cloth taking up to six months to complete, which makes such work very expensive to buy.

1) Traditional *tjanting* with beaten copper cup and bamboo handle
2) Modern *tjanting*

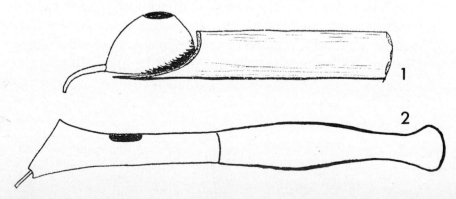

Detail of Indonesian batik: stylized Bird-of-Paradise motif (Semen pattern)

Detail of sarong, probably from north or east Java: stylized lotus flowers and vines in indigo, brown and red on cream ground

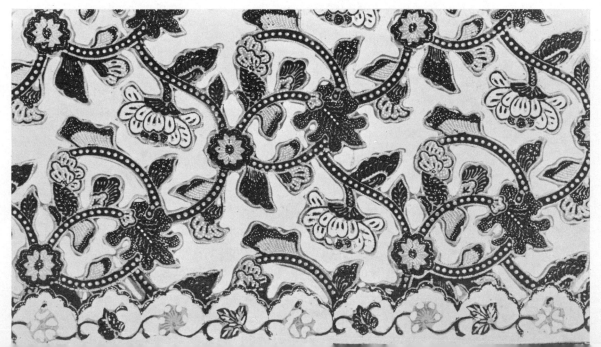

It takes long practice to become skilful with the *tjanting*, so the little girls begin to use it when they are very young. Children of Indonesia learn the art of batik at their mother's knee, just as girls in other lands learn to knit or embroider. The girls, returning from school, squat on the ground within the circle of village women who sing and gossip as they work around a smouldering charcoal fire that warms the wax. In front of each worker the cloth is suspended on a low frame (see below). With one hand under the cloth and the other holding the *tjanting*, the children soon become as skilful as their mothers at following the intricate patterns, which in time become so familiar to them that no preliminary drawing is necessary. Large in-fillings are done with a brush, and both sides of the material must be carefully waxed before the first dipping in dye.

The cloth passes to the men for dyeing in its first bath, which is usually indigo blue. After drying, the men scrape off the first wax-paste and the cloth is returned to the women, who apply another lot of wax to the areas which are to remain white or indigo during the next dyeing operation. This second dye is

LEFT Old woman from Surakarta using the *tjanting* to draw wax outline
RIGHT Group of Indonesian women working with *tjantings* on *tulis* (hand-drawn) batiks

usually red-brown, obtained from sago-bark. It turns the white areas reddish-brown and the indigo areas dark-brown, unless the indigo has been covered with wax-paste to keep it blue. The unusual 'Horses and Chariot' wall hanging (see below) is a rare Indonesian batik in these traditional colours. It is rare because Indonesian batik is almost solely made for clothing.

After steaming has taken place to set the dye, the cloth is boiled thoroughly to remove all the wax paste, the wax being reclaimed for further use.

This whole process is known as *tulis batik,* meaning 'hand-painted'. Very little of the cloth we see today is produced in this tedious way. With the advent of cheaper cottons from Japan in the nineteenth century, a faster means of production for batik became necessary.

THE TJAP

At this time, a new method was developed in which a block with an intricate wire pattern on its underside was designed.

Indonesian hanging: *Horses and Chariot,* in traditional indigo, brown and red-brown (sago-bark dye) on cream ground

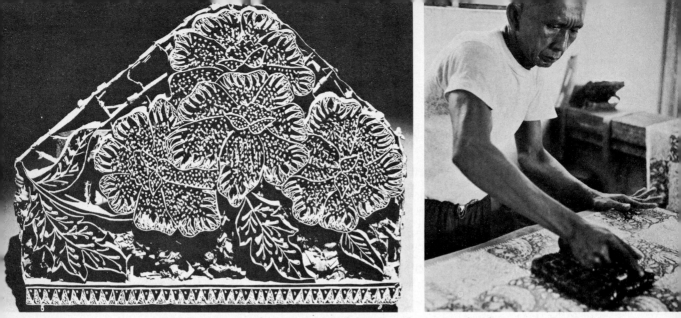

LEFT A *tjap* used for stamp-printing to accelerate production
RIGHT Using a *tjap*. Printing must be matched on both sides of cloth. *Tjap* printing is always done by men

This became known as a *tjap*. With this the wax is stamped on to the cloth much more quickly. It is still painstaking work, however, as the design must match perfectly back and front; it is heavy work, too, done by the men. Most of the estimated forty million yards of batik produced each year is printed by this method.

For both methods, much labour goes into the preparation of the cloth, which is soft cotton. Pre-shrinking, steeping in coconut oil, boiling and starching is done before waxing begins.

Batik has always been vital as a village industry, bringing a little money and employment to peasants between rice-planting and the harvest. But in Indonesia, Malaysia and Singapore today the batik industry is of tremendous importance, and production has reached an industrial scale. From country villages it has progressed to city factories—but, as so often happens, it has lost much of its significance on the way. Synthetic dyes are used now, and although much simpler and faster,

8

they lack the subtle colour distinctions that belong to dyes of regional origin. Mass production by the *tjap*-printing method has imitated patterns merely to satisfy public demand and the tourist trade. Different designs appear every week, and, while this keeps the market lively, finer points of the ancient art are being lost.

Fortunately, some of the old, traditional batiks have been kept for generations, and are worn on special occasions. Moreover, both Indonesia and Malaysia have recognized the importance of this indigenous art, and it is being fostered and encouraged as never before in the light of their new, independent nationalism. Artists are being commissioned by their respective governments to produce batik murals depicting the life of their people, thus promoting an ancient craft to the status of a fine art equal to any in the world.

The people of Indonesia and Malaysia are extremely proud of the rare beauty of their fine hand-made batiks, and it could be said that the ancient art is undergoing a renaissance which will ensure its survival, preserving it from the fate of so many ancient handcrafts now lost to us in this modern, machine-made world.

LEFT Detail from a batik wall covering with Bima hero from the Hindu epic saga still current throughout South-east Asia. *Photo: Hoechst*
RIGHT Section of modern Indian sari in negative-positive design. Squares of white, orange and dark-blue on silk

2 BATIK TODAY

Batik first reached the Western world when Dutch East Indies traders took batiks home with them to Holland in the seventeenth century. From there, interest in the art spread throughout Europe, being taught as an art form as well as a unique method of fabric printing.

Today, there is a world-wide revival of interest in the manual arts. It seems that in this age of automation, the need to make and own hand-made articles is part of the search for our own vanishing identities. So batik has become popular in England, America and Australasia, as well as in Europe, because it is an important and vital activity of man. It is a technique that expresses very effectively an individual, personal statement. There is tremendous pleasure in wearing a garment wholly designed and printed by your own hand; in creating a wall-hanging especially to suit a certain room; or making a lamp-shade, cushions, blinds or curtains that are just what you want. Batik is a craft with so many applications that you never run out of ideas, and, because it does not need large or complicated

10

equipment, it can be carried out in the home or schoolroom without great expense.

One of the loveliest aspects of batik is its translucency. When batiked fine cotton or silk is used to make a lamp-shade or screen, the light filters through it just as it would through stained-glass. But its texture is delicate, soft, and immensely decorative, with the added attraction that it can be easily hung or transferred to another position at will.

Today, interior designers use texture to a greater degree than ever before. The soft, matt glow of a batik wall-panel or screen adds depth by contrast, or enhances the harmony of a room, acting as an interesting foil for conventional paintings or prints.

It is only during the last twenty years that artists in Malaysia (and recently in Indonesia) have developed the ancient fabric-printing technique to suit the demands of modern painting. The development of strong chemical dyes that can be used cold, much as water-colour is used for painting, has resulted in a new and exciting art technique. Tradition has made batik a natural form of expression for the people of Indonesia and Malaysia; in Kuala Lumpur alone, there are at least fifty artists using this medium.

Because art is a truly international language, artists all over the world have discovered this new and exciting medium and have adapted it to their own particular environments or styles. In this way, new international friendships and understanding are developing between East and West—another vital link in the chain of world friendship is being forged.

11

3 BASIC EQUIPMENT

For Waxing

1 Because wax is inflammable, heating with a naked flame should be avoided if possible. An electric frypan or hotplate, thermostatically controlled, is ideal. If wax is heated in any other way, use an asbestos mat beneath the pan—and then, keep the melted wax hot by standing the container in a larger pan of hot water.

2 The table on which you work should be covered with plastic sheeting or newspaper, unless it has a resistant surface which can be scraped clean of wax.

3 The cloth to be waxed should be pinned to a frame so that it is about four inches clear of the table surface. Four lengths of 3″ x 2″ softwood, which can be adjusted to any size by fixing with four 4″ clamps, are most convenient. You can, however, improvise with an old picture-frame, an upturned stool, or drawer. And it is possible to lay your cloth directly on the table surface, if the latter is covered with waxed paper.

4 Blocks of paraffin wax or candles; beeswax if possible.

5 *Tjanting* (if available).

12

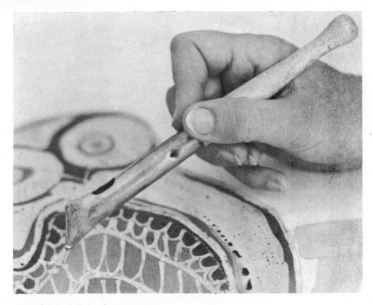

Working with the *tjanting*

6 Brushes. For beginners, I suggest three brushes: a small water-colour brush, a ½″ size, and a 2″ size of the ordinary household paintbrush type. There may be old brushes about your house, which, although not good enough for fine work, would be ideal for waxing of broader areas. Once used for wax, they are best kept only for this purpose, as it is too difficult to remove the wax each time they are used. They will harden when cold, but soften up the next time they are dipped in hot wax.

For Dyeing
1 Polythene sheeting.
2 Rubber gloves.
3 Plastic bowls or buckets.
4 Plastic or glass measure and plastic spoons.
5 Cold-water dyes.

13

Preparing the Cloth

For best results, use only pure cotton or silk : avoid synthetic materials. The finer the material, the finer the crackle (see pages 24-7). Heavy burlap or towelling will need waxing on both sides. Drip-dry surfaces should be boiled to remove the resistant substances.

It is advisable to wash and iron the fabric before you begin. A light starching helps to control the flow of wax.

Final removal of the wax is usually done by ironing the cloth between sheets of white or brown paper. This process is illustrated in the section of photographs describing how to make a cushion cover (page 21). A moderately hot iron will not harm your work, and is, in some cases, the correct method for setting the dye. Where it is desirable to use washable dyes for clothing, however, final boiling is recommended in the case of Dylon dyes. In this case, alternate immersion in very hot, then cold water, will facilitate removal of the wax. Dry cleaning will remove the residue of wax remaining after this.

SCARF DESIGN

This easy one-step scarf design is a good project with which to begin. An ideal size for a scarf is 32″, and if you can buy a scarf with the edges already hand-rolled, this will save you work. Choose white or some pastel shade, in silk or cotton.
1 Either pin the scarf out over a frame, or lie it flat on waxed paper. (The wax will be less liable to stick to this.)
2 Heat the wax, and using a 2″ wide brush, draw your pattern in large, loose swirls of wax from the well-filled brush.
3 Immerse the scarf in a cold-dye bath and allow to dry either by hanging it on a line out-of-doors or flat on a newspaper,

The Artist's Work-bench
Assorted equipment:
Plastic dye-bath and rubber gloves
iron and brown paper
cleaning spirits
electric fry-pan

beeswax, paraffin, candle
measuring spoons and spare jars
jars and packets of powder dyes
brushes and *tjantings*
softwood framework which can be fixed
with four clamps

with plastic sheeting underneath.

4 Iron out the wax by pressing with a moderately hot iron. There should be a good layer of brown paper or newsprint underneath the material, and a single sheet on top. Papers should be renewed as they become soaked with wax.

In the illustrations below and opposite the original scarf square was aqua-blue, and after dipping in vermilion, the finished design was aqua and purple. A yellow scarf immersed in vermilion would become yellow and orange.

A second waxing and dipping in a darker colour dye will produce a three-colour scarf. There are an infinite number of colour combinations which can be developed from three or four primary colours.

If there is too much wax left in the scarf after ironing, it should be dry cleaned, either professionally or by putting it through cleaning fluid yourself. (Be very careful when using inflammable spirits.)

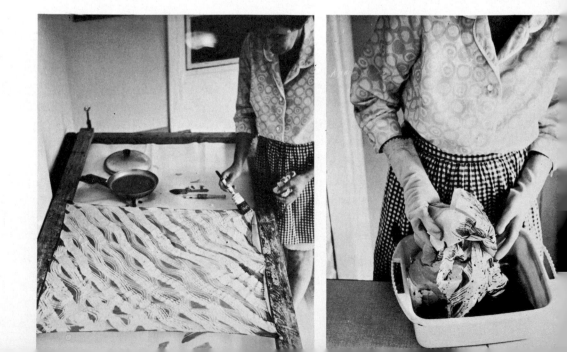

MORE ABOUT WAXING AND DYEING

Waxing

The wax should be hot enough to penetrate the cloth. If it lies on the surface, dye will run under it and the results will be smudgy. Check on the wrong side of the material after waxing, and wax that too if it looks patchy. Temperature of the wax will vary with different fabrics: generally it needs to be between 200°-300°. The boiling point of water is 212°, so caution and supervision of children is very necessary.

When the brush is immersed in hot wax for the first time the bristles will fuzz out. Press them back into shape on the sides of the pan until all air is expelled.

Hold a pad under the brush to catch any drips, and with a full brush begin painting with good, even strokes. If the wax looks 'milky' it is not hot enough: it should look clear as it penetrates the fabric. At first, you may find it difficult to control—it may overrun lines, but with experience you will learn to work with the brush about ¼″ inside the line to allow for this.

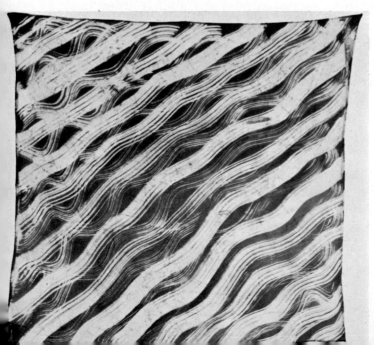

FROM LEFT TO RIGHT
Applying wax to scarf with 2″ brush
Dipping crumpled scarf in dye bath
Final effect when wax is ironed out

17

Dyeing

Make sure, first of all, that you have a big overall to cover yourself for this work, and wear rubber gloves.

Because hot water would melt the wax, dyeing must be done in cold water. In America, several good dyes especially produced for batik are obtainable at art stores. One type of dye is in liquid form; its colour is set by exposure to sunlight, which makes its use in batik design a fair-weather process. Most modern dyes are very intense synthetics requiring the addition of salt or vinegar (acetic acid) to them when they are mixed with water.

ICI Procion dye is the type most readily available in the U.K. and Australasia. The German company of Farbwerke Hoechst also produce fast cold-water dyes. In both cases, the process necessary for fastening the dyes is fairly complicated, and is not recommended for beginners, although they can help more practised batik workers to obtain very striking results. Full instructions for their use are available from the companies concerned, and from some art stores.

For beginners, ordinary household dyes obtainable at chemists and hardware stores are adequate. They should be mixed according to directions, but not diluted too much. Gilseal and Dolly Dyes are examples of this type of household dye, and if these are made up in the quantities of one packet of dye to one quart of water and stored in glass jars, they will keep for several months. They can be further diluted with cold water if necessary when you come to use them, and are quite suitable in this form for wall-hangings or lamp-shades, for example—but not for anything which requires washing. Dry cleaning will not affect them, however.

For articles such as clothing, which will need washing, Dylon (cold) dyes are suitable if the directions are carefully followed.

At the end of the batik process, the makers recommend steeping in boiling water, which permanently fixes the dye.

In the case of Procion dyes, which are very penetrating, rewaxing is often necessary between the second and third dyeing. Examine your work well, and if it shows signs of flaking off or over-cracking, then go over it again with wax before its next immersion in dye.

Printing pastes or screen printing dyes can be used for painting of selected areas which have been 'islanded' with wax. Colour felt pens are also useful for highlighting and touching up, although their use can spoil the batik if it is too obvious.

Paste Resist Method for Young Children

As no heating is necessary for this process, it is a safe method for young children. Some Javanese, African and Indian fabrics are dyed in this way, by using paste-resist made from rice or sago flour. It is possible to substitute plain flour for this.

1 Add flour to water until the paste is still thin enough to squeeze from a plastic squeeze-bottle, but thick enough to form a solid line on the cloth. (An old plastic detergent bottle will do for this process.) You will find that 1 tablespoon of flour to ¼ pint of water are the approximate quantities needed.

2 Make a direct drawing or a tracing on the cloth in charcoal or crayon. Cover this outline with the paste and allow to dry completely.

3 Dye can now be painted on the areas as desired. It is necessary to use a thicker printing paste for this: Permaset, Reeves, or other screen-printing pastes are suitable.

4 Allow each colour to dry and cover with more paste before proceeding with the next colour.

5 After final drying, the paste can be scraped free and the cloth ironed to set the dye.

A MULTI-COLOURED DESIGN

After trying your hand at the simple, one-step scarf design described and demonstrated earlier, you will have absorbed the basic ideas and will now be ready to try a design using several colours.

This will immediately make clear to you the developmental colour processes that make batik such an exciting medium. As new colour is added, it affects the colour preceding it. Study colour plate 1. I have demonstrated here a very simple cushion design using four graduated circles. By the time colour and crackle (see pp. 24-7) are added, the end result is most effective (see illustration of finished cushion opposite). In black-and-white photographs, I have demonstrated the accompanying actions that produced the results shown in colour plate 1.

1 The drawing for the design is prepared in charcoal directly on to the cloth, or else drawn first on paper, and then traced on to the cloth. Any sign of pre-drawing will spoil the finished work, so a lead pencil or ball-point pen should be avoided. Lightly used charcoal or a crayon in a light tone blending with the major background colour will not be visible.
2 Waxing-in is done with a small brush, changing to a larger size for broader areas.
3 The material is crumpled well to achieve a good crackle effect, before the last immersion in black dye.
4 The wax is ironed out after the final drying, using newsprint or brown paper.
5 This shows the completed cushion, with its interesting crackle effect.

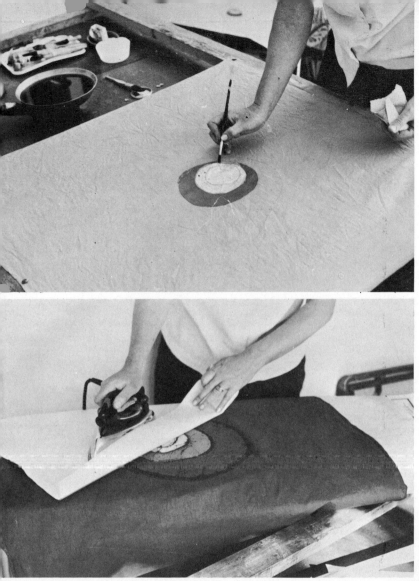

ABOVE Waxing with small brush
BELOW Ironing out wax, using white or brown paper

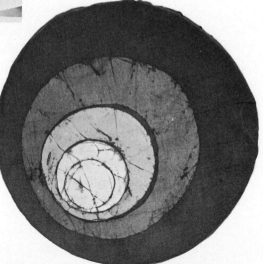

Completed cushion cover

4 CREATING DESIGNS

Every art medium has its own particular qualities suggesting certain subjects for design, composition and treatment. The design you choose will depend on the article you want to create. If you intend to make a wall-hanging, you will have to consider the composition exactly as you would for a painting. You may have some flower, bird or abstract form in mind. It is best to begin with something simple, with clean, uncluttered outlines on a plain background. The batik medium itself is so interesting that an over-complicated design can spoil its effect.

With experience, colour and design can be allowed to develop as you advance from step to step, allowing free and spontaneous expression, but beginners are well advised to do a full drawing in colour, thinking carefully about which parts of the whole they want to retain with wax in each colour.

Circles, lines and dots can be made by the simple candle-dripping method described on page 28. By holding the cloth at an angle and allowing the wax to run down, a striking willow-tree effect, for example, can be obtained.

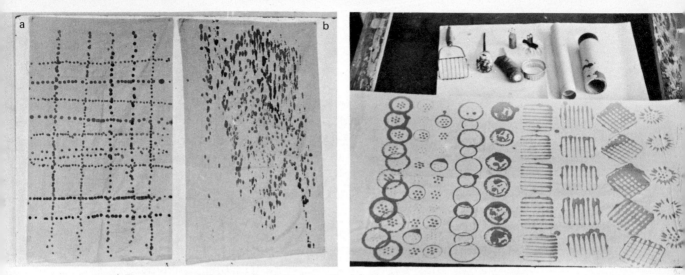

LEFT Patterns made by candle-dripping: a) with cloth in horizontal position; b) with cloth in slanting position
RIGHT Home-made stamps (improvised *tjaps*) and their effects

Kitchen utensils such as a scone-cutter, potato masher, or corks, or a flower-holder, as well as cloth wound round the end of wooden sticks can be used to add variety. In doing this you are in effect making your own simple tjap. The photograph above gives examples of the effects of different stamps such as these, with the implements shown alongside the material.

A string design, made by dropping a piece of string on to the cloth to form abstract shapes, can help you to begin. Drawing around your own hands and waxing in the outline can produce a surprisingly satisfying batik. The crackle effect, after you have crumpled the cloth and dipped it in a dark colour, suggests the veins of the hands.

23

One of the most inspiring sources of design ideas is provided by our natural surroundings. All about you there are natural objects ready to be used. Pictured opposite is a quickly made collection of objects from around the house and garden, all of which would adapt very well for use in batik design. Sometimes just one section of them will give a pleasing abstract pattern.

In most countries of the world there is some source of native art, often very ancient, which can be adapted effectively to the batik medium, with very decorative results. In America there are Indian and Mexican designs; in Europe, ancient cave-paintings, the rich folk patterns of Scandinavia, the decorative Moorish influence in Spain. In New Zealand, the Maoris are masters of intricate design which lends itself readily to adaptation into modern work. In Australia, there is an almost untapped source of aboriginal art, both cave and bark painting as well as ornamental decoration found on weapons and everyday objects. Cave paintings are ideal, with their irregular rock background, for adaptation to the batik medium, when the crackle can suggest the rock surface. On the opposite page is a batik design inspired by an ancient Mimi cave painting from Northern Australia. (Dancing Mimi women are also depicted on the Australian dollar note.) Also pictured is a bark painting with a typical criss-cross X-ray pattern, again very appropriate for adaptation into batik designs.

CRACKLE

This descriptive word, which I have already used a number of times throughout the text, describes that particular characteristic of batik which makes it unique: the distinguishing feature by which we recognize the batik process apart from any other type of fabric printing.

24

Designs from nature

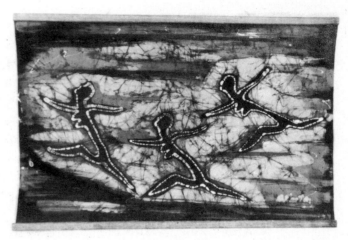

Hanging inspired by Mimi cave painting from Northern Australia

Aboriginal bark painting from Northern Australia: flying foxes

25

TO19864

'Crackle' is really the result of an accident in batik manufacture. As the cloth is dipped in the cold-dye bath, the wax cracks, causing veins of darker colour to marble the lighter areas. The full effect of this cannot be judged until the wax is ironed out or removed by boiling or solvents: the result is a general unifying effect that connects and relates pattern with colour. For the same reasons, a painter in oils or water-colours uses a 'master' colour as an undercoat, allowing patches of it to show through later applications of paint. In the case of batik, however, this crackle is the result of dipping in the final bath of dark dye, as we have seen. There is an alternative technique used in India and China, where the cloth is completely waxed and crackled first. Then, after removing the wax, the design is superimposed on this marbled background.

Some artists prefer to have very little crackle in their designs, if any, and they achieve this by increasing the amount of beeswax or other hardener added to the paraffin wax. Most modern artists, however, have taken the happy 'accident' a step further, creating their batik paintings in such a way that the crackle becomes a special textural feature; in fact, an integral part of the composition. By trial and error they learn to control and induce the effect to a certain degree, but inevitably the accidental aspect remains as well. This, in fact, is what makes batik painting so intriguing and exciting: the final removal of the wax can evoke delight or disappointment, depending entirely on the success or failure of the crackle effect.

The amount of crackling allowed to develop is a matter of personal choice, and this, in turn, is obviously affected by the design you have chosen. Simple, strong forms can take more crackle than finely drawn, intricate designs. It is necessary to establish the correct balance between these two so that the final

Pelican: heavy crackle

Academic Owl: medium crackle

effect is harmonious. I like to contrast areas of strong crackle with plain areas for emphasis in large wall-hangings.

The Christmas Tree hanging described and illustrated on pp. 28-9 makes use of the decorative qualities of crackle, and the crackle also creates a unified effect between all the colours on the tree, and its surrounding background.

27

MAKING A WALL-HANGING: CHRISTMAS TREE

This is an ideal group activity for supervision by parent or teacher.

1 The children begin by drawing with crayon a simple cone-shaped Christmas Tree. For the design illustrated, yellow material was used.

2 After the wax is heated, they cover all the area around the tree and its base with wax, using brushes.

3 Candle-wax is then dripped on to the tree area only, in both the direct-drop (illustrated below) and the sloping position. (See also photographs on page 23 and on back of dust-jacket.)

4 The yellow cloth is immersed in red dye, resulting in an orange-red tree with yellow spots of light on it. The area around the tree remains yellow with bright orange crackle. The fabric is then hung to dry.

5 More candle dripping on the tree preserves some of the red dye. The tub at the base of the tree is covered with wax at this stage, so that it remains solid red in colour.

LEFT Children dripping candle wax on to Christmas Tree design
RIGHT Children immersing Christmas Tree design in dye

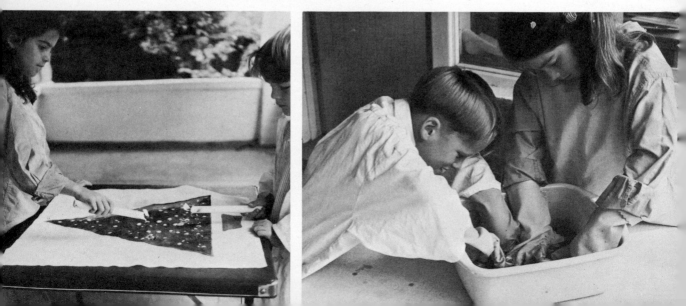

6 A second dipping in purple dye produces a dark background for the red and yellow spotted tree, and darker veins of crackle appear in the surrounding yellow area.

8 The wax is ironed out.

9 The children then have fun sticking glittering sequins and stars on the tree with glue.

10 To add to the festive appearance, loops of matching gold ribbon are sewn to the upper and lower edges of the hanging, after the edges have been turned for strength.

11 1″ dowelling covered with gold foil is inserted through the the loops, and a sash of gold silk added.

HOW TO HANG YOUR BATIK

Before attempting to hang a batik, it is essential to make sure your hanging is absolutely square—you should, therefore, always tear your cloth to begin with, to get it straight. Any contrast in threads used for hemming can mar the finish, so do your best to match the basic background colour of the design —or else hem your material first, so that the thread takes up the dye with the batik. In this case, of course, it will match perfectly and be invisible. A good ½″ hem is advisable at the sides for strength.

The lower and upper edges of the hanging can be treated in various ways. By turning a casing hem, a dowel can be run through, or a 1″ or 2″ batten painted or stained a suitable colour can be stuck on or stapled.

A third, more decorative method is described in the section on the Christmas Tree hanging. Loops of ribbon were sewn at regular intervals along the upper and lower hems, and dowelling inserted through these loops (colour plate 5).

Silk cord in matching colours can be used to suspend the finished work, or, for a small hanging, a brass curtain ring threaded through a 2″ length of ribbon and attached to the centre of the batten is simple and effective.

A batik can also be framed like any other picture, but because of the striking effect light lends a batik when it shines through it from behind, I prefer to leave them unbacked. In general the less obvious your treatment for hanging, the better.

LEFT *Acropolis:* done with *tjanting* for fine detail. Brush used for background. In several shades of blue on white
RIGHT *Heron:* brush work, pale-green on deep blue-green ground

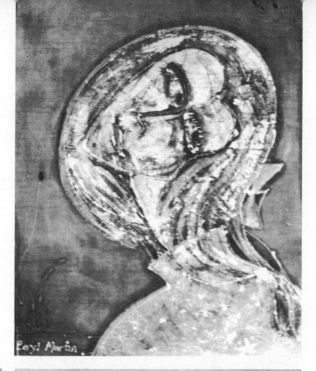

RIGHT *Head of Girl:* done with *tjanting* and brush. Aqua and purple on pale-blue ground
BELOW LEFT *Peace Conference:* doves done with *tjanting* on aqua and lime-green ground done with brush strokes. Final dipping in dark-brown dye gives emphasis and crackle
BELOW RIGHT *Arches by Moonlight:* done with brush only in several shades of blue and purple on white ground

MAKING A MAN'S TIE

Men's ties call for special pattern treatment; both personal taste and current fashion demand consideration.

Suggested materials: cotton poplin, sailcloth, shantung, silk, linen or lawn.

1 You will need a strip of material 54″ long and twice the width of the broad end of the tie (approximately 6″). Tear the fabric straight to begin with, tapering it afterwards by folding it in half down the centre line. It is a help to unpick an old tie to use as a pattern. This may contain a lining strip that can be re-used. Otherwise, cut a strip of bias unbleached cotton 15″ long and 1″ wide for the lining strip, and attach this to the centre seam of the tie, beginning at the broad end. If you prefer, the tie can be fully lined, or stiffened at the front with iron-on backing.

2 Batik the tie length before making up. Fine dark crackle in the final dyeing is the desired effect here.

LEFT Baby's feeder in pink and dark-blue on white towelling
RIGHT Dress neckline designed in white and orange on dark-grey

3 Dry cleaning is necessary for thorough wax removal either before or after making up the tie.
4 When pressing, it is advisable to insert a flat ruler up the front of the tie to prevent a ridge appearing down the centre front, created by the back seam.

The colour illustrations in this book show other articles of clothing you can make, in addition to tablecloths, bedspreads, curtains and blinds.

MAKING A LAMP-SHADE

Translucency is a very important factor in designing a strip of material for a lamp-shade, so keep your colours as light as possible. Dark crackle looks most effective over them. Give special consideration to other patterns in the room where the lamp will be; for instance, I would avoid a patterned shade in a room which contains floral curtains or upholstery, unless you can ally the shade with them in colour or design. Graduated stripes or abstract swirls in matching colours might be possible. *Suggested fabrics:* fine lawn, silk.

1 For simple making-up, choose the straight barrel shape for your lamp-shade.
2 Buy top and bottom lamp-shade rings, obtainable at hobby shops or handcraft sections of large stores, and stiffened heat-resistant lining.
3 Cover the rings with 1″ white tape, winding it around them.
4 Choose the lamp base with care, looking for good balance and a plain surface that will not detract from the interest of your shade design. Be careful about proportions of shade to base. Usually they need to equal each other in height; width will depend on the thickness of the base.

5 Tear the length of material to ensure straightness, and carry out batiking in the usual way. (Material should be $3\frac{1}{7}$ times the diameter of the rings, plus $\frac{3}{4}''$ for overlap.)

6 Iron out the wax, leaving as much in as possible in this instance to preserve the surface and help to keep it clean.

7 Cut stiffening $\frac{1}{2}''$ less than fabric at both upper and lower edges, and $\frac{1}{4}''$ less at one end. The latter allows for the rough edge of the fabric to be lapped under the stiffening and glued down.

8 Using PVA glue, run this along top and bottom edges, sticking the material to the lining and in each case leaving $\frac{1}{4}''$ overlap free.

9 Secure the ends together in the same way, overlapping and glueing down the extra $\frac{1}{4}''$ to neaten the edge. (It is possible to buy an adhesive lining which facilitates the glueing process.)

10 Run glue around the previously taped edges of top and bottom rings. Carefully insert the rings, one at a time, into place, resting each on top of the stiffening inside the shade.

11 Roll the remaining $\frac{1}{2}''$ of fabric over the glued rims, tucking the rough edge under the wire.

12 An alternative method to that described above, and one which beginners may find easier, is to glue the edge of $1''$ ribbon to the edge of the fabric, folding this over the wire and glueing it again on the inside.

For examples of several lamp-shades, see colour plate 3.

If you have followed carefully the simple, practical advice given in these pages, trying out the suggested easy scarf and cushion designs, and then perhaps attempting to make a wall-hanging, a tie, or lamp-shade, you should be well on the way to a real understanding of the beautiful art of batik. As with any art

medium, constant practice will increase your skill and con-
fidence, so that your designs will gradually become more
ambitious. Good luck to all batik beginners!

ERRATUM

Instruction 2: for washed, read waxed

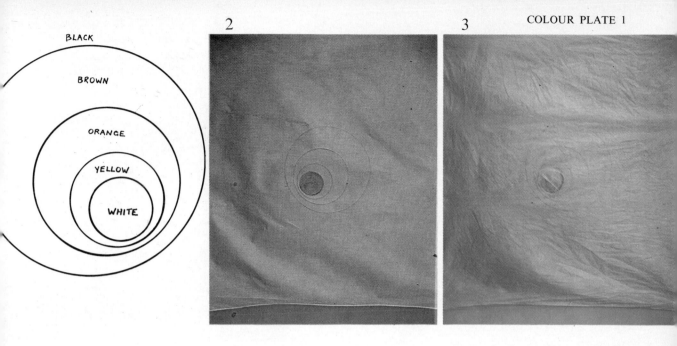

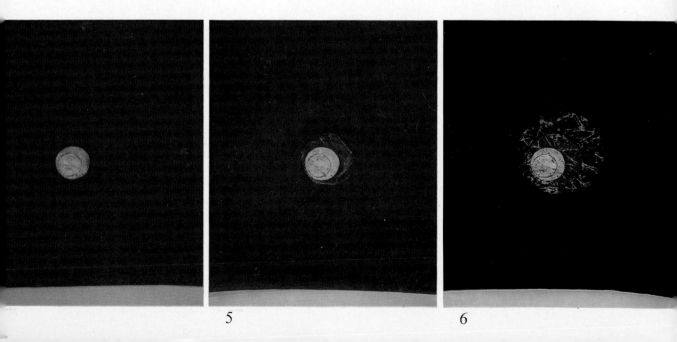

1 Prepared charcoal drawing
2 Centre circle, which is to remain white, is washed
3 Cloth is now dipped in yellow dye, and after drying, the area to remain yellow is waxed
4 Cloth is dipped in red dye, and after drying, the area to remain red is waxed
5 Cloth is dipped in brown dye, and after drying, the area to remain brown is waxed
6 Final immersion in black dye. This photograph shows how the hanging looks before ironing out

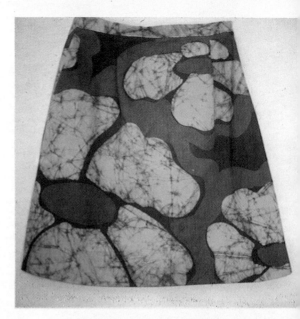

BELOW LEFT Dress: heavy ribbed cotton
BELOW RIGHT Overblouse: cotton poplin
RIGHT Girl's short skirt: cotton poplin (by Amanda
Martin)

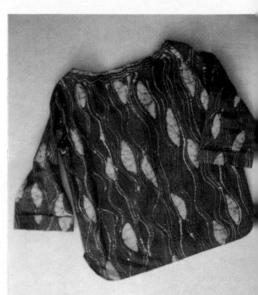

TOP RIGHT Girl's matching dress and hat (by Lenna Symons)

TOP LEFT Blue hostess skirt in silk organza; pink skirt in silk chiffon

LEFT Group of lamp-shades

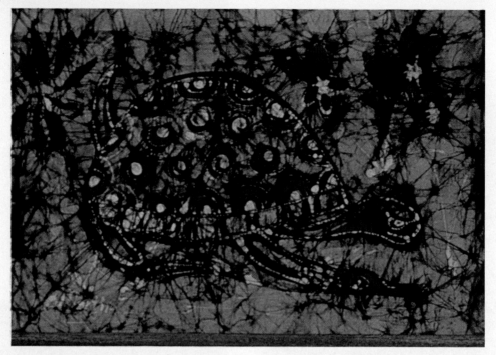

Tortoise

Ocean Deep

Christmas Tree

Mermaid

Owls

Coolies' Dance

Land of Totem

Firebird

Happy with Mother: Chuah Thean Teng. *Photo: Straits Times*